MR. WEATHERBY'S TEA PARTY

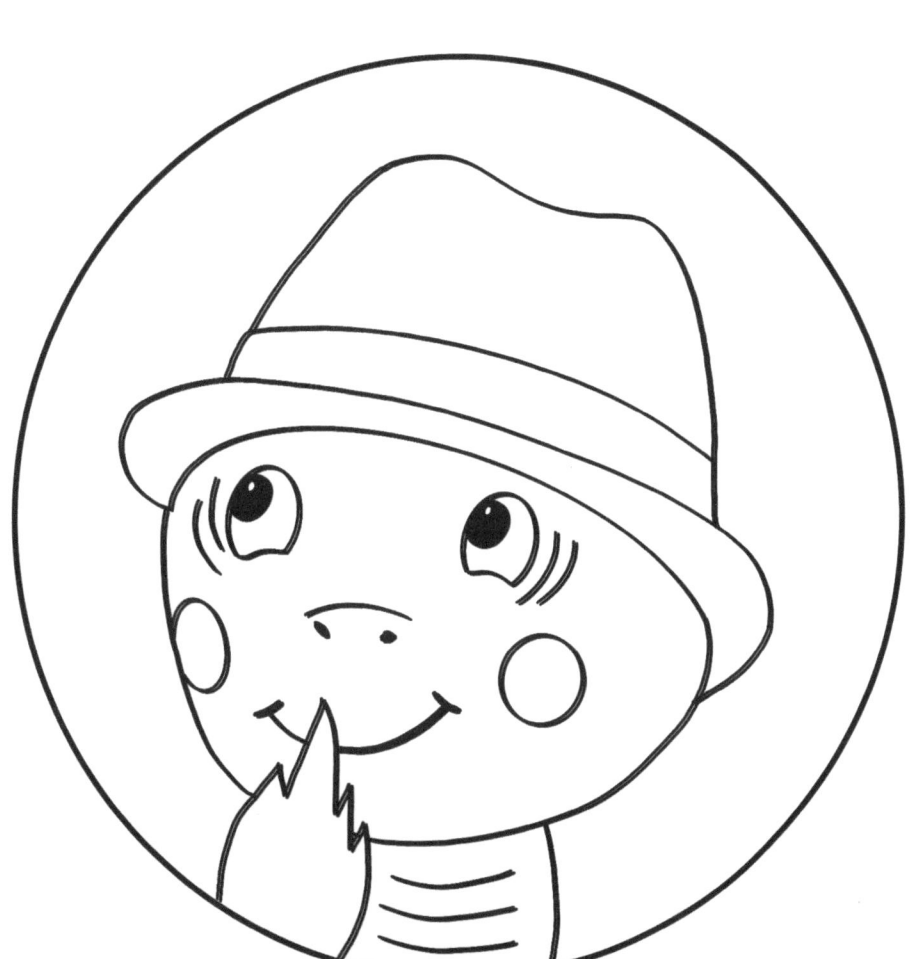

LOUISE DOUGHERTY

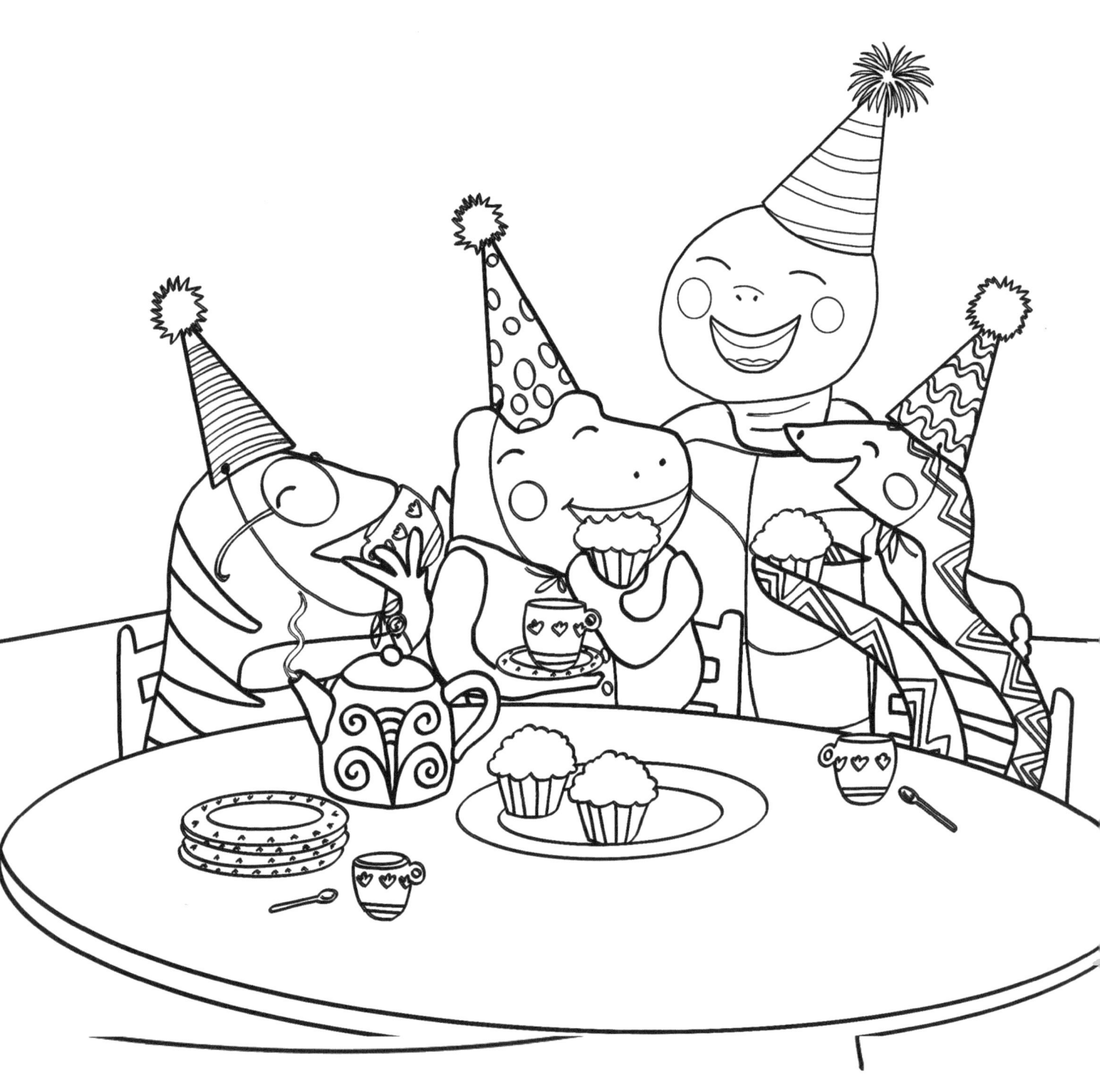

ON A SUNNY DAY WITH CLEAR BLUE SKIES, A SPARK LIT UP IN MR. WEATHERBY'S EYES.

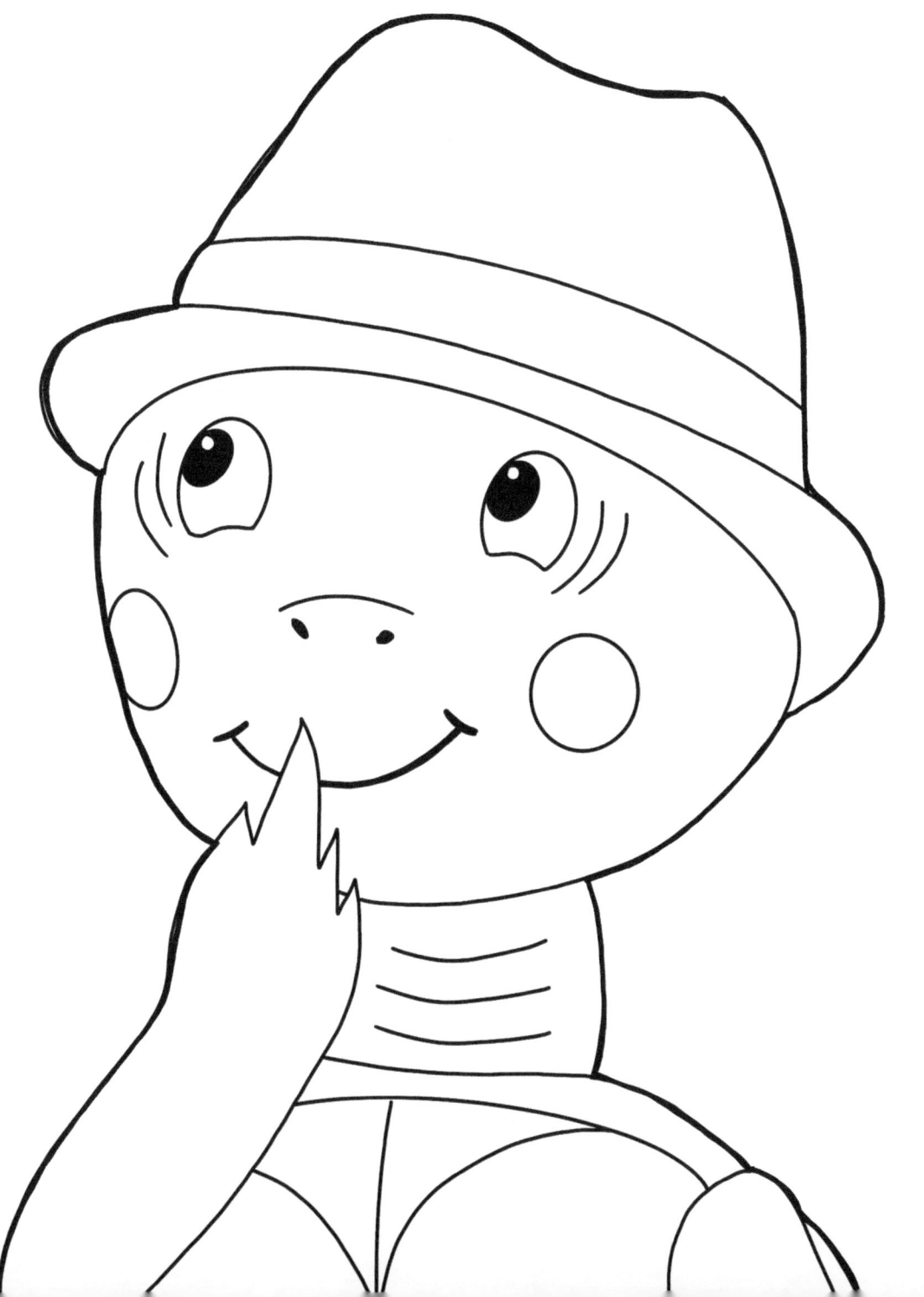

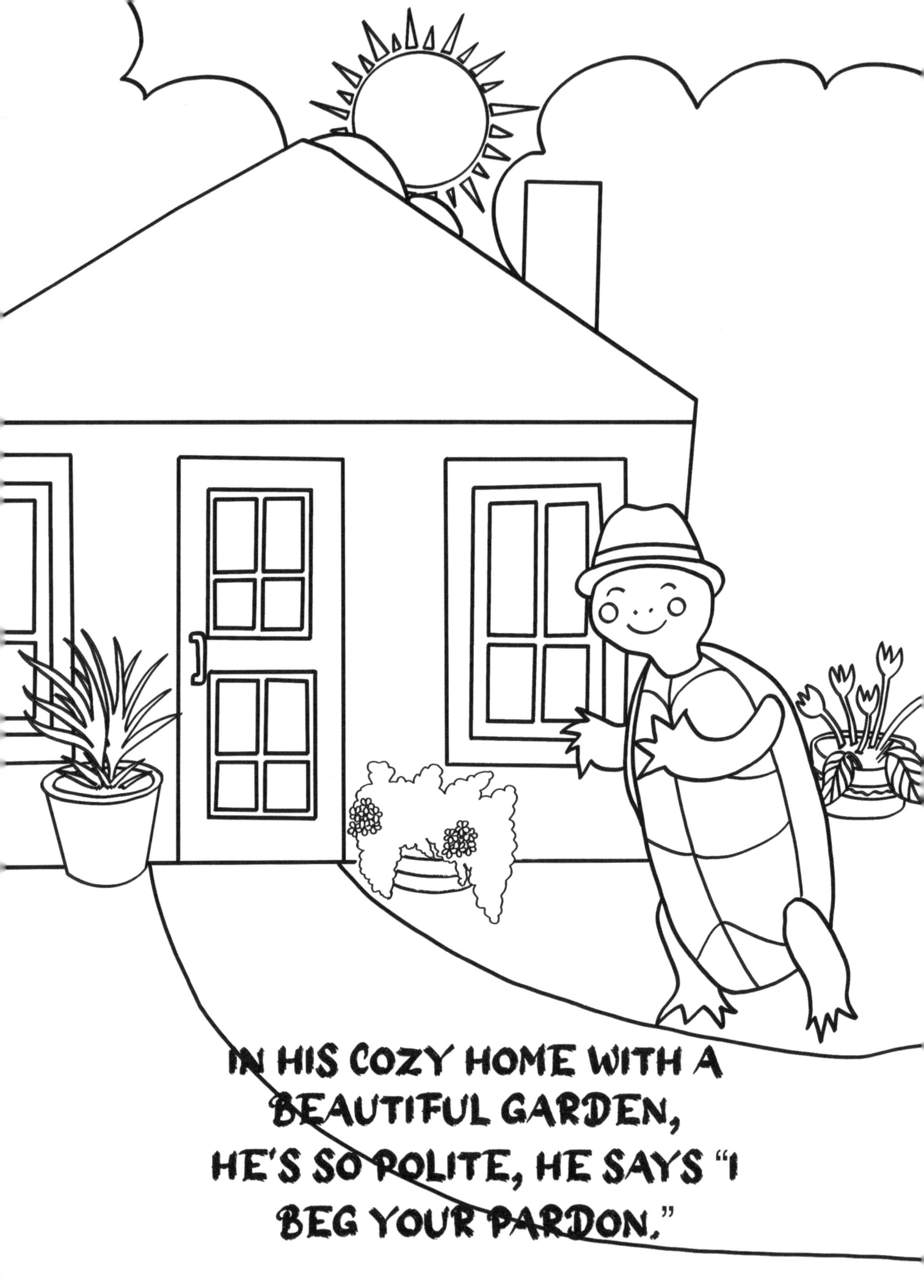

IN HIS COZY HOME WITH A
BEAUTIFUL GARDEN,
HE'S SO POLITE, HE SAYS "I
BEG YOUR PARDON."

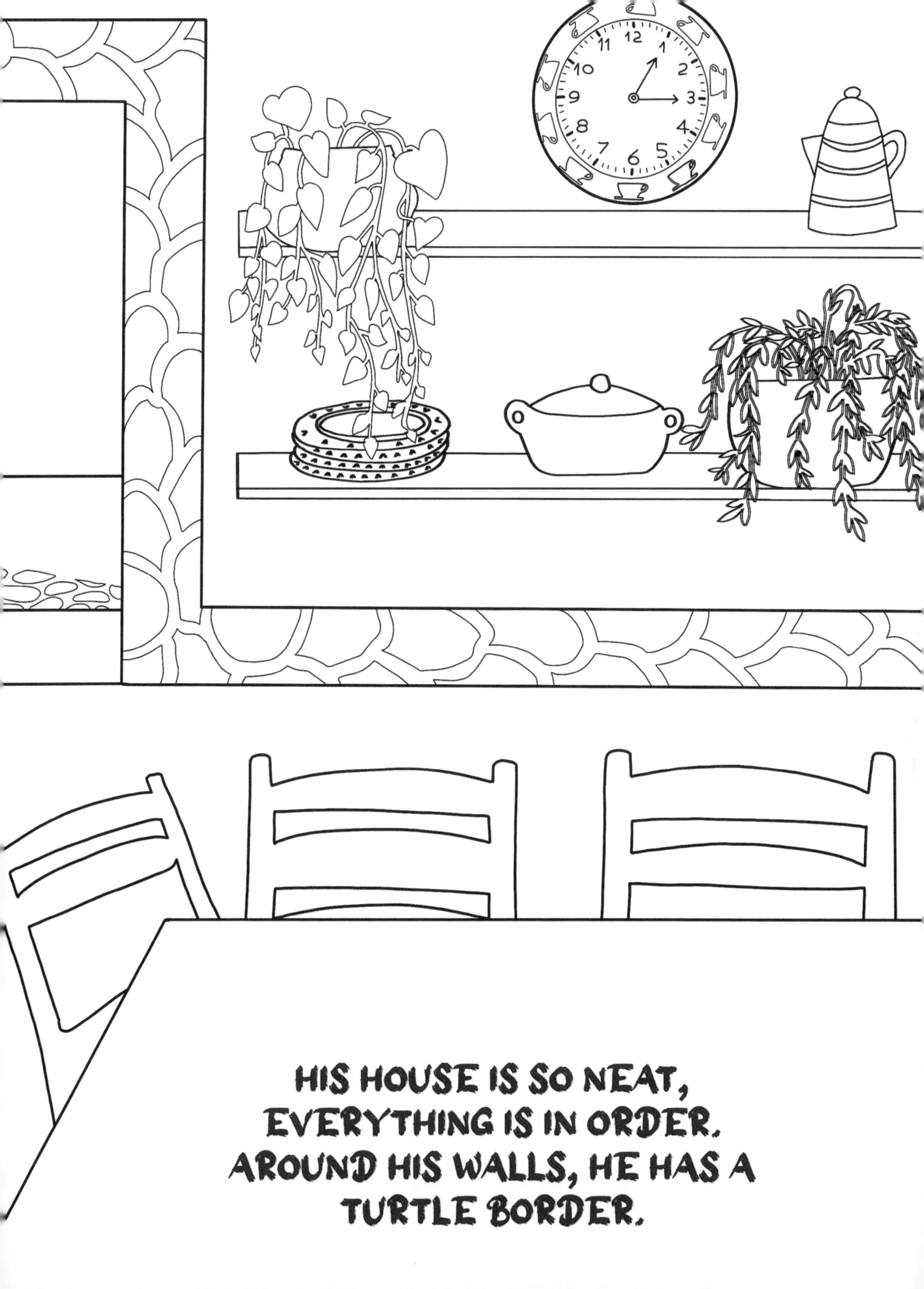

HIS HOUSE IS SO NEAT,
EVERYTHING IS IN ORDER.
AROUND HIS WALLS, HE HAS A
TURTLE BORDER.

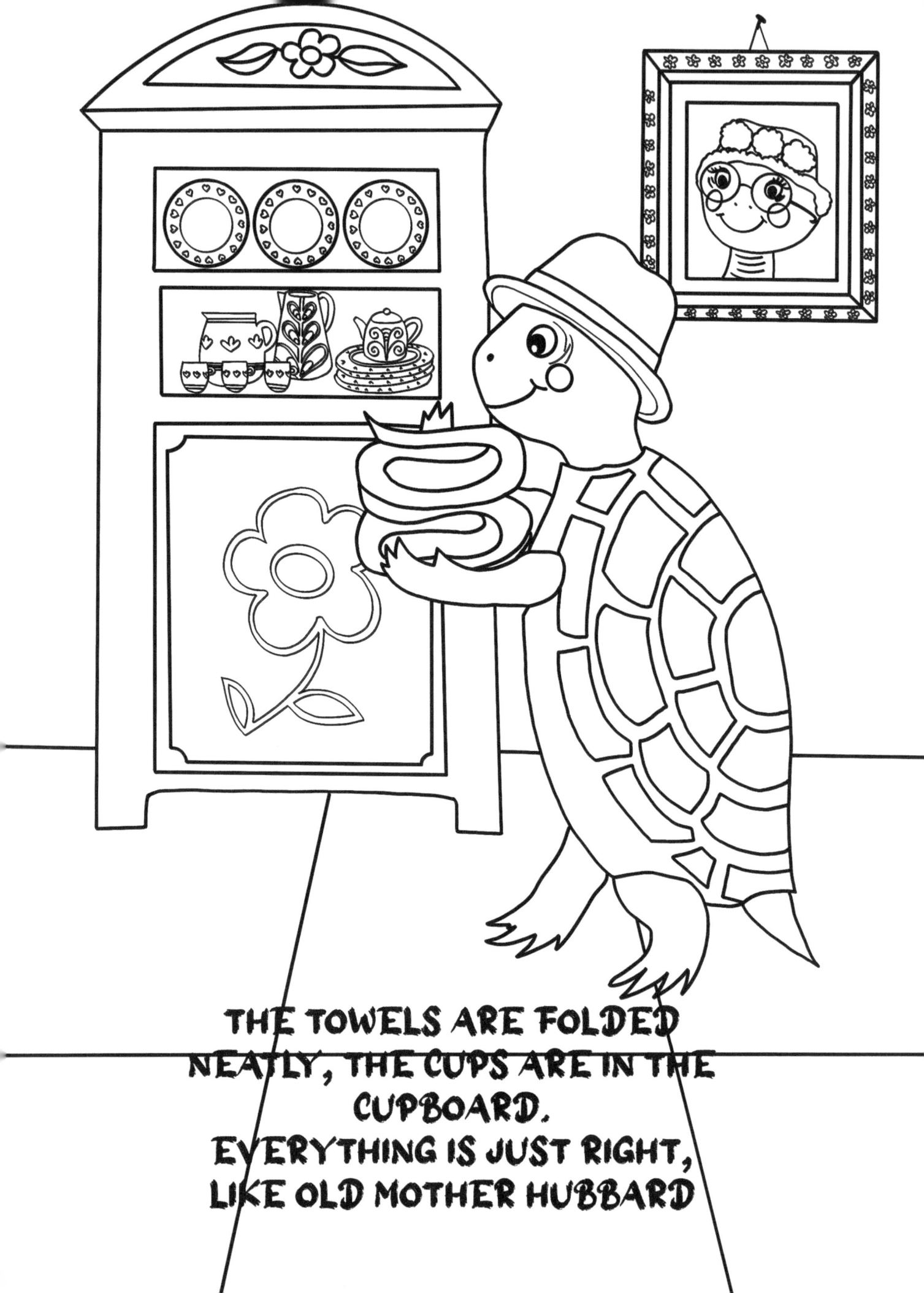

THE TOWELS ARE FOLDED
NEATLY, THE CUPS ARE IN THE
CUPBOARD.
EVERYTHING IS JUST RIGHT,
LIKE OLD MOTHER HUBBARD

WHAT SHOULD I DO ON THIS FINE DAY?
I WILL HAVE A PARTY, AND INVITE FRIENDS OVER TO PLAY.

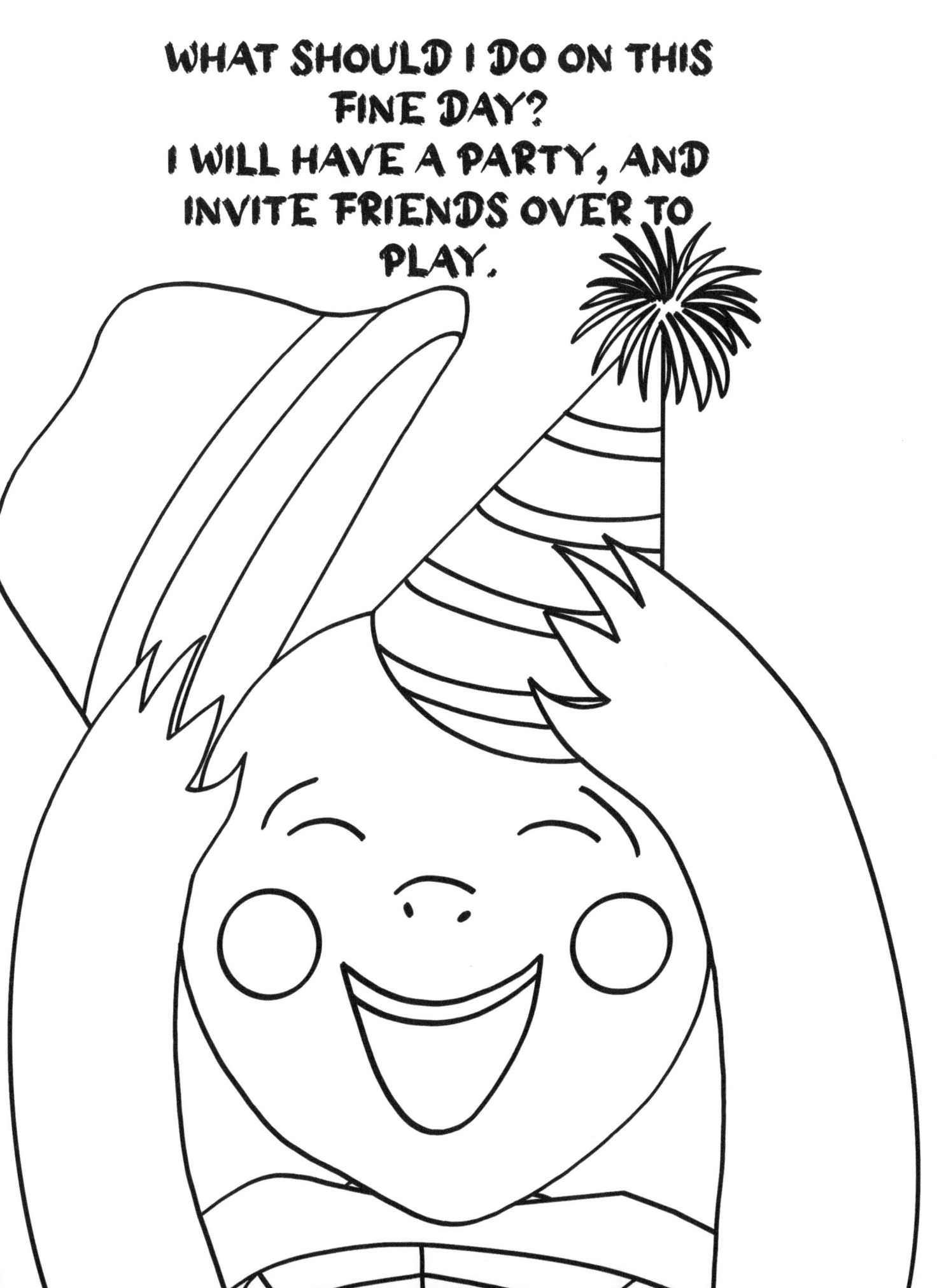

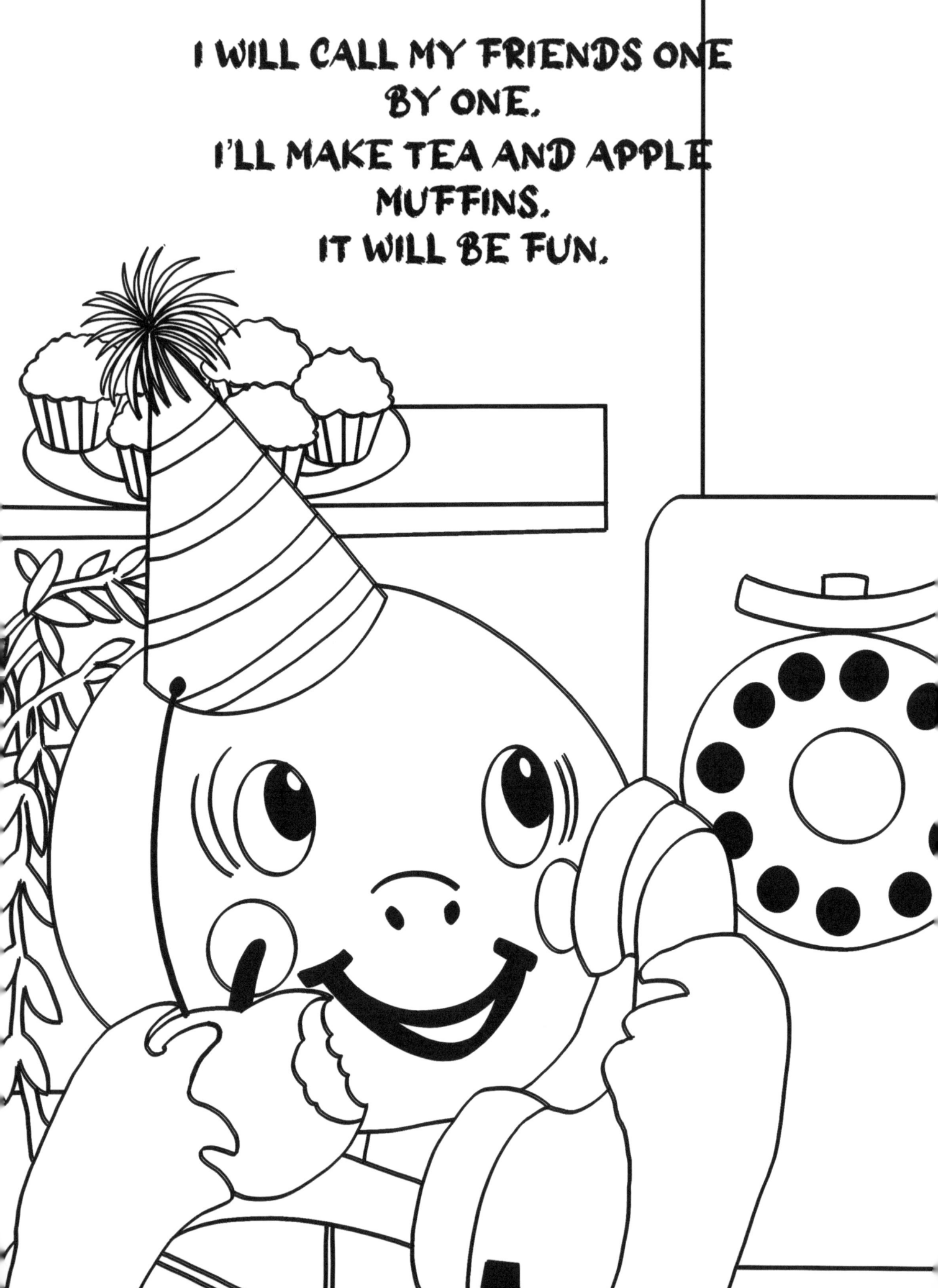

THE FIRST TO CALL IS MR. FROG.
CAN YOU COME TO A TEA PARTY?
WE'LL HAVE TEA AND APPLE
MUFFINS, AND IT WILL BE
HARDY.

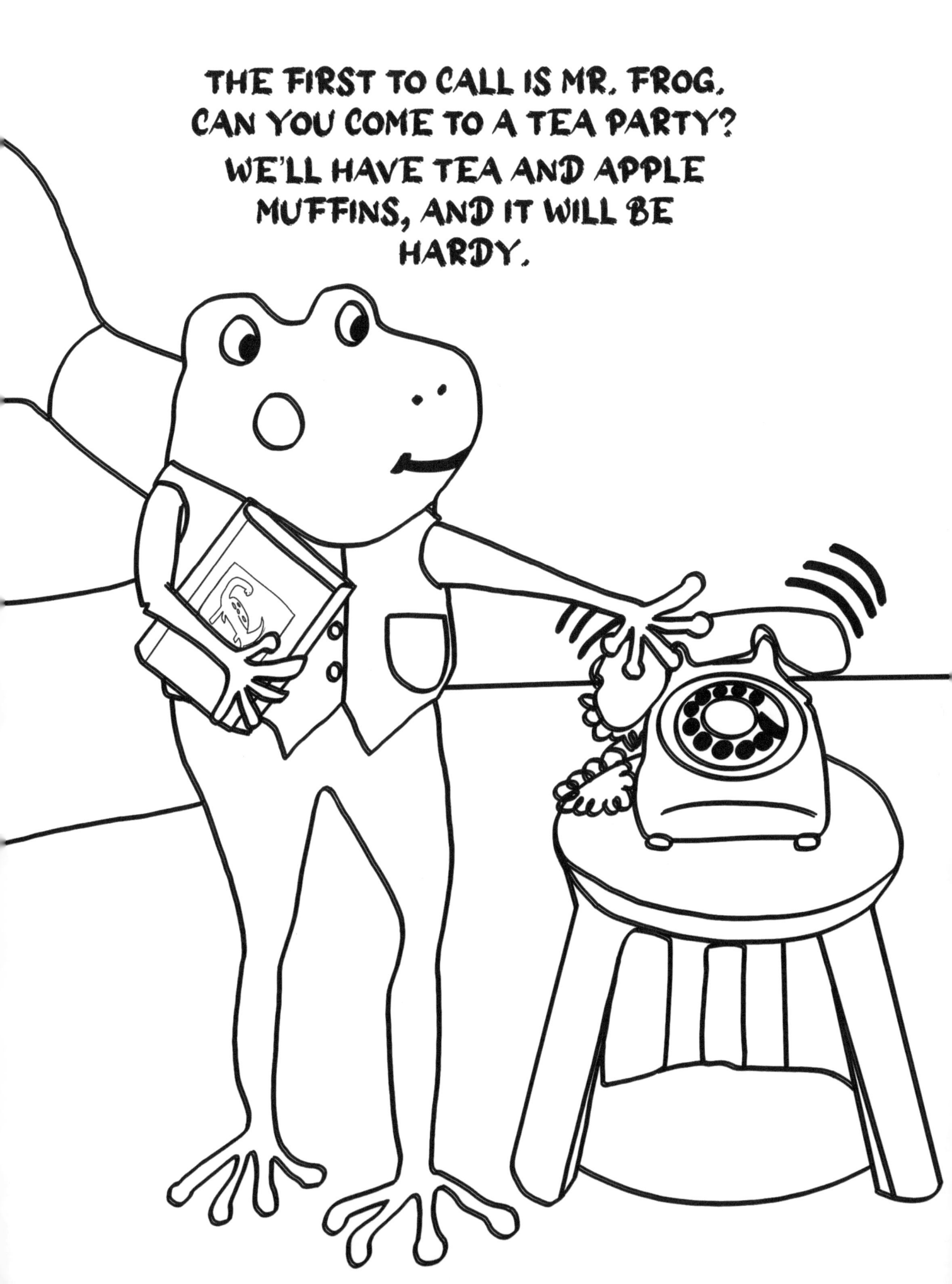

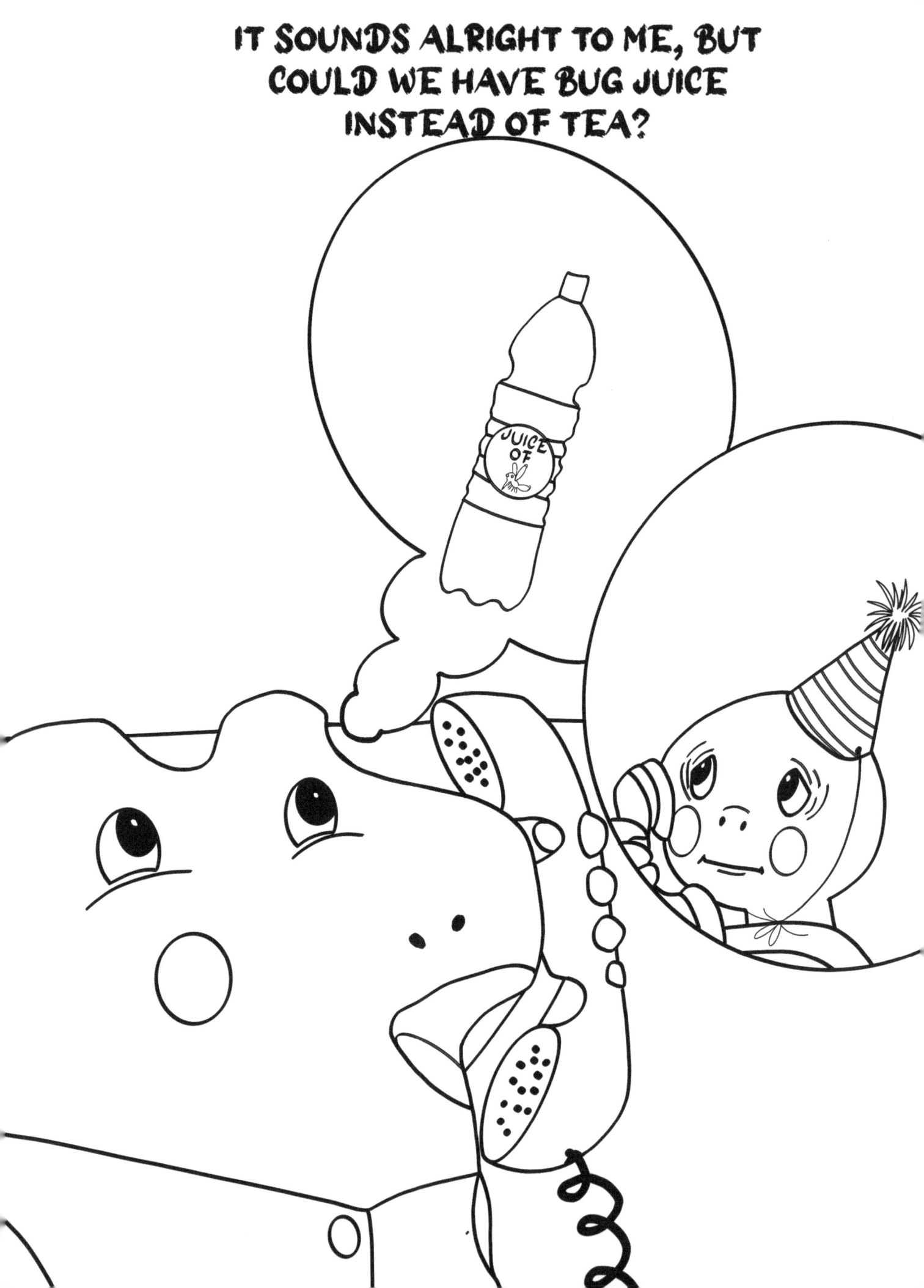

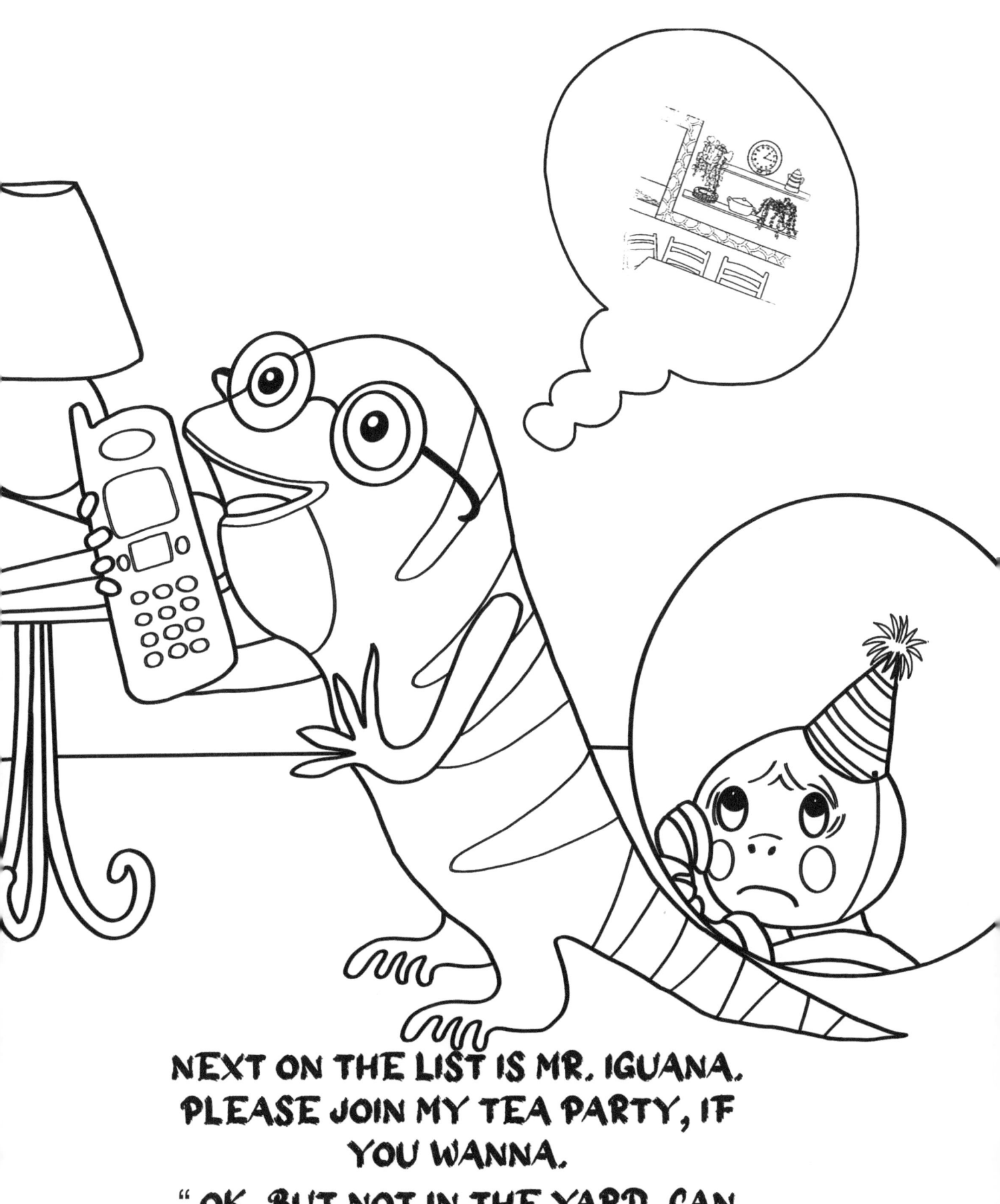

NEXT ON THE LIST IS MR. IGUANA.
PLEASE JOIN MY TEA PARTY, IF
YOU WANNA.
" OK, BUT NOT IN THE YARD. CAN
WE SIT INSIDE IF IT'S NOT TOO
HARD? " SAID MR. IGUANA.

NEXT TO BE CALLED WAS MR. SNAKE, PLEASE COME TO MY PARTY, APPLE MUFFINS I'LL BAKE,
"I'D LOVE TO, BUT IF IT'S NOT TOO MUCH TROUBLE, CAN YOU INSTEAD MAKE AN UPSIDE-DOWN APPLE BUBBLE?"

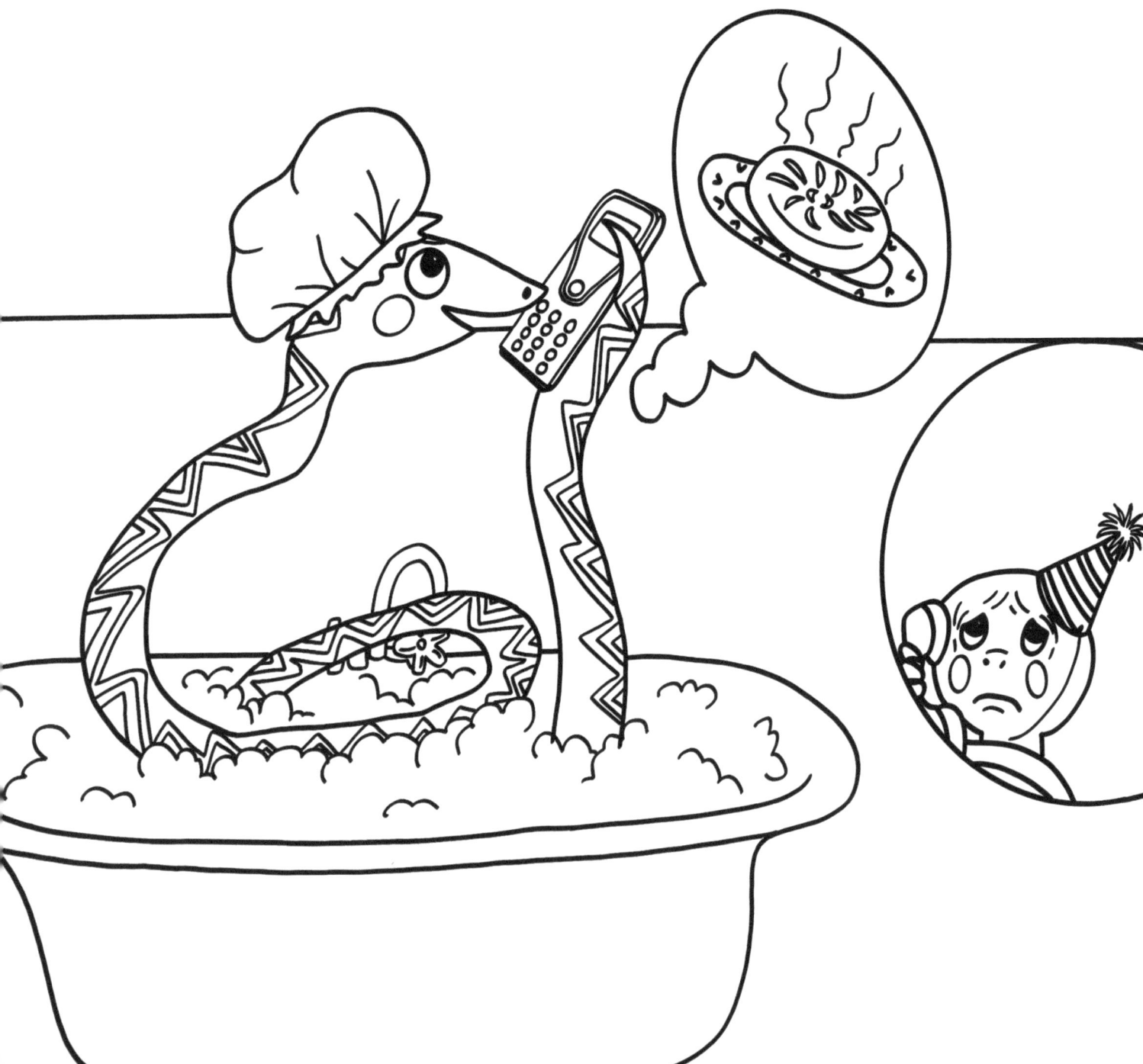

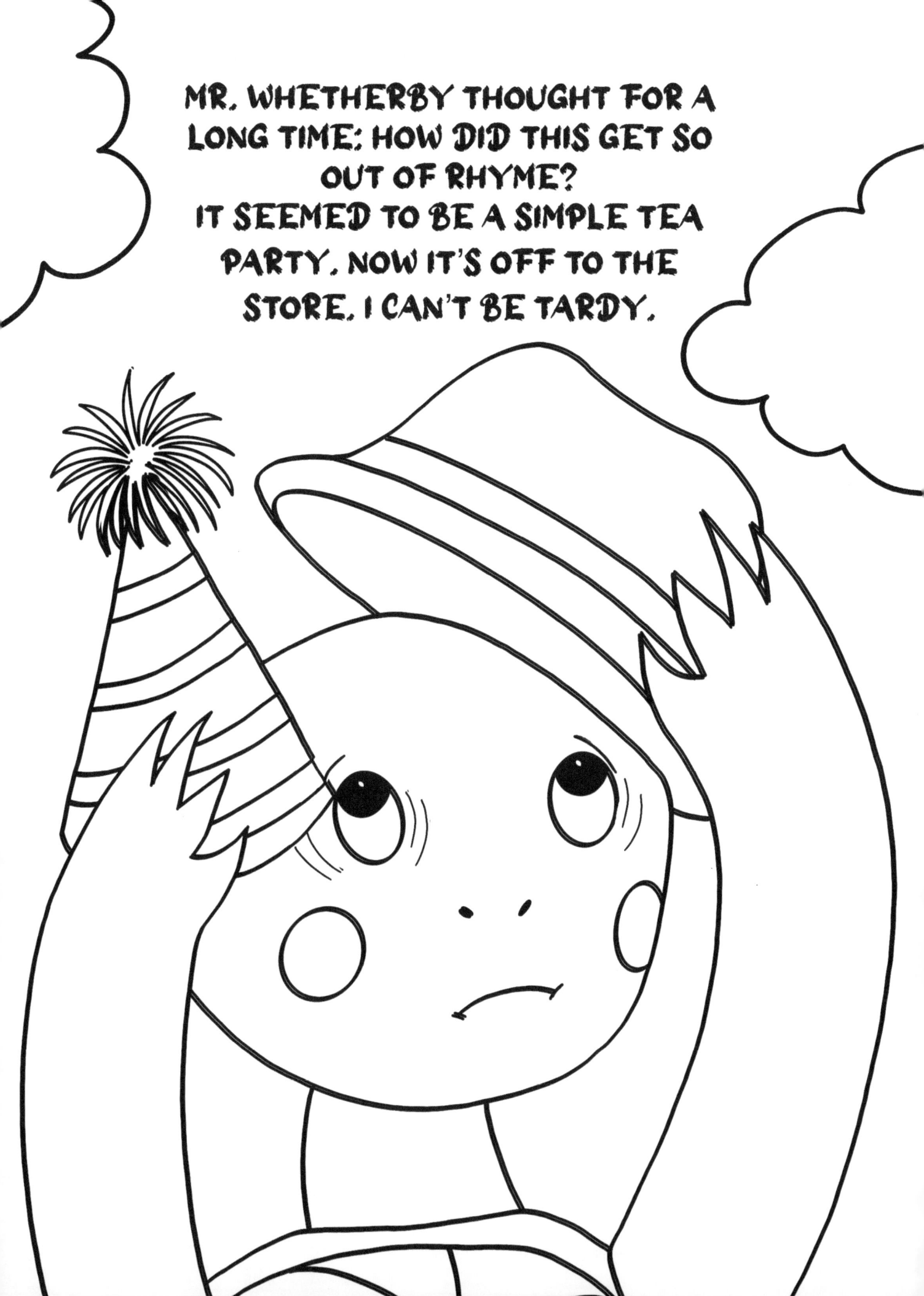

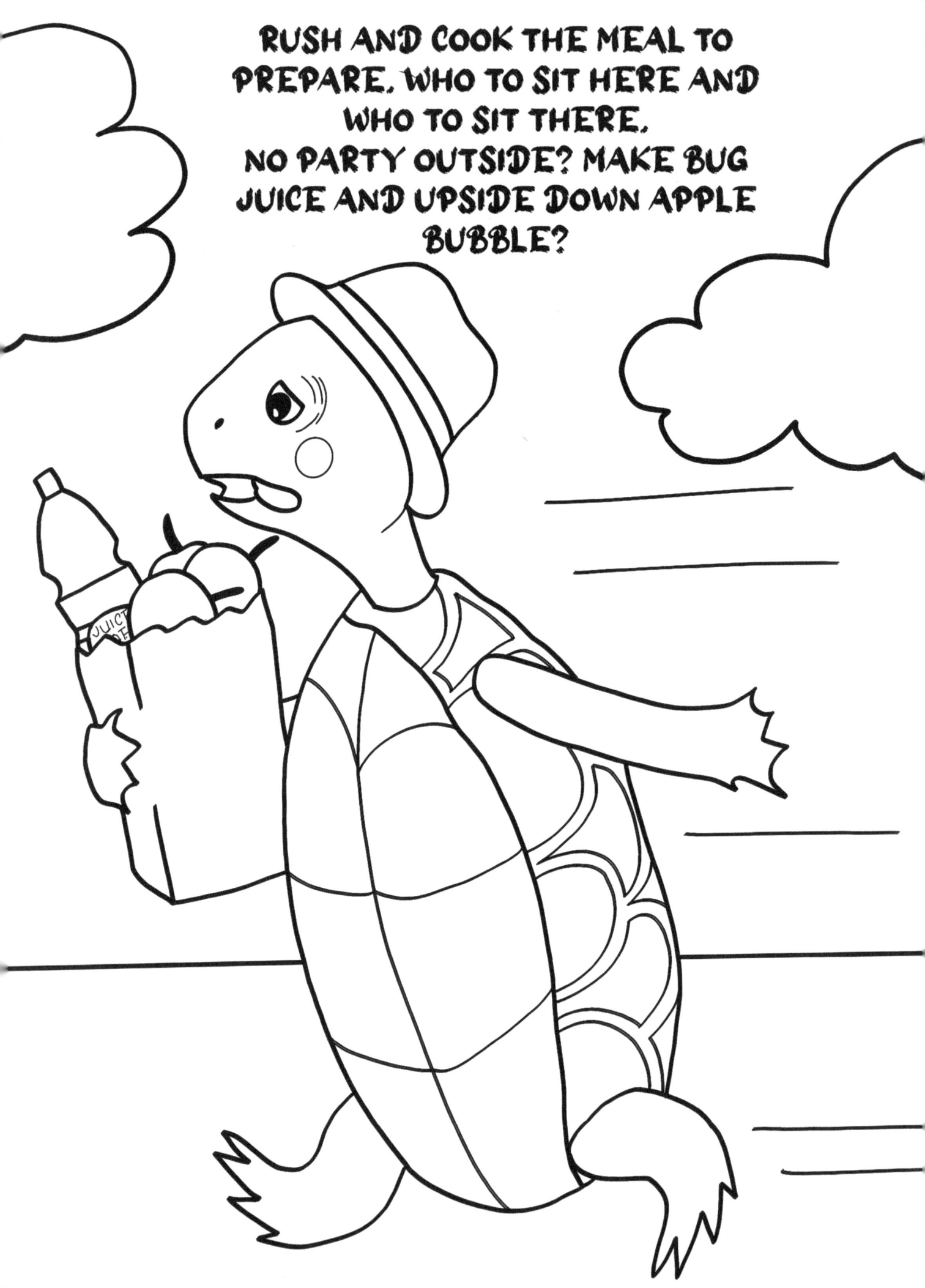

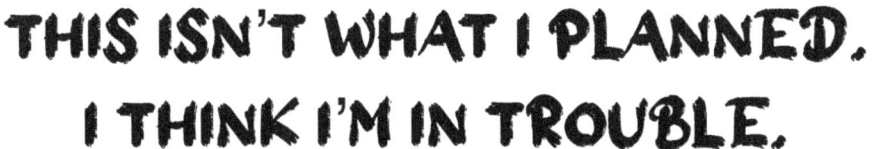

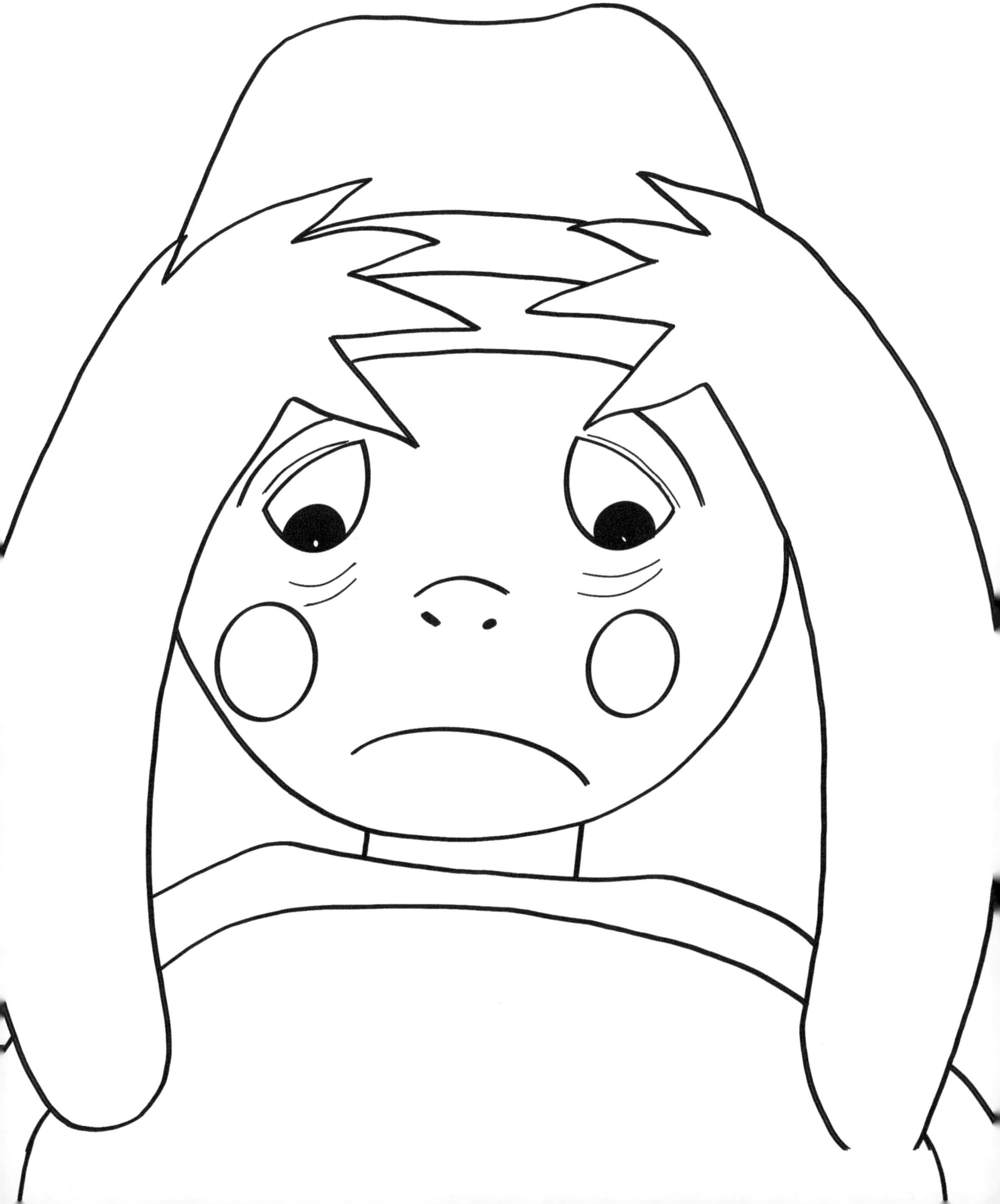

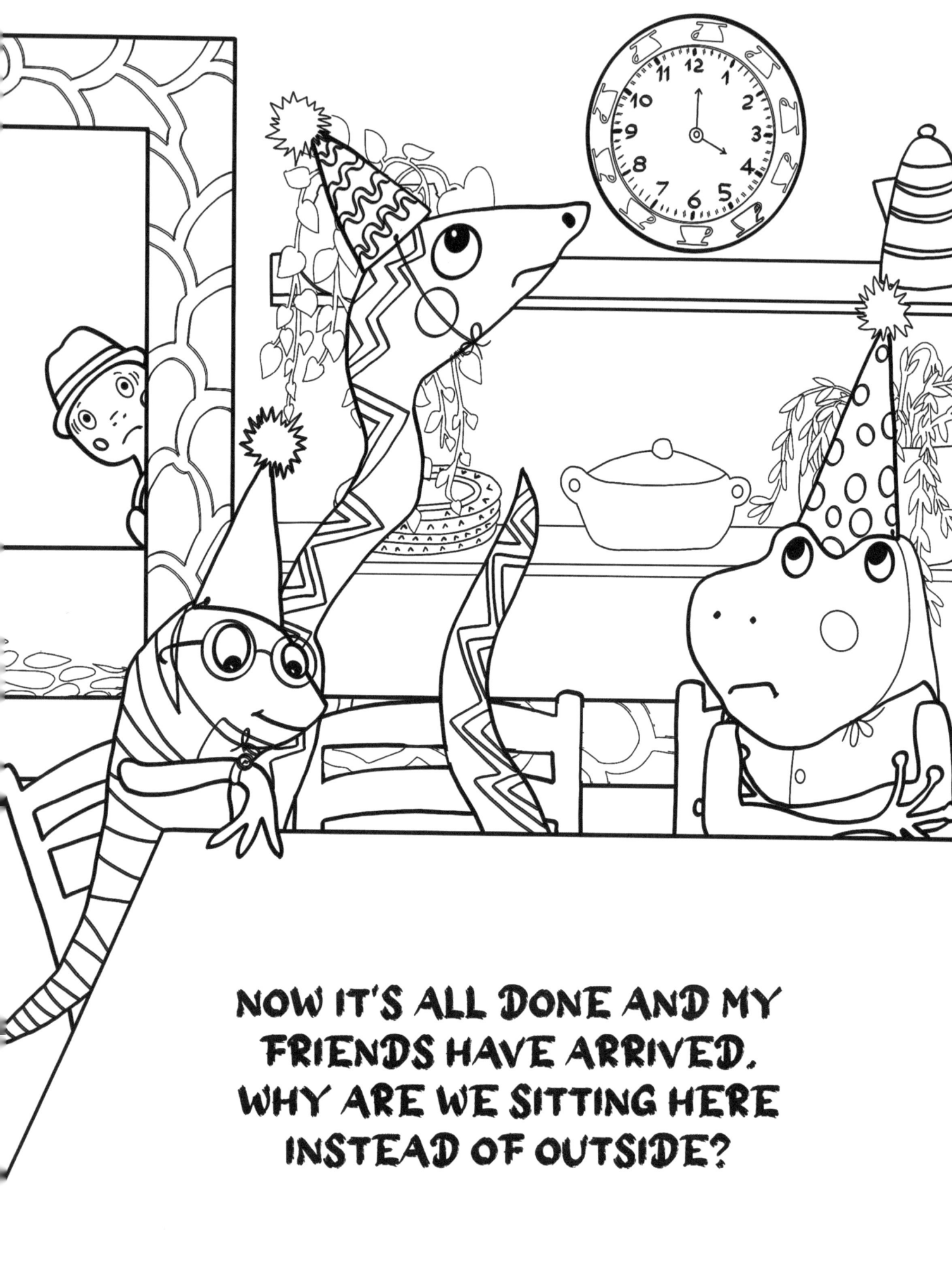

NOW IT'S ALL DONE AND MY
FRIENDS HAVE ARRIVED.
WHY ARE WE SITTING HERE
INSTEAD OF OUTSIDE?

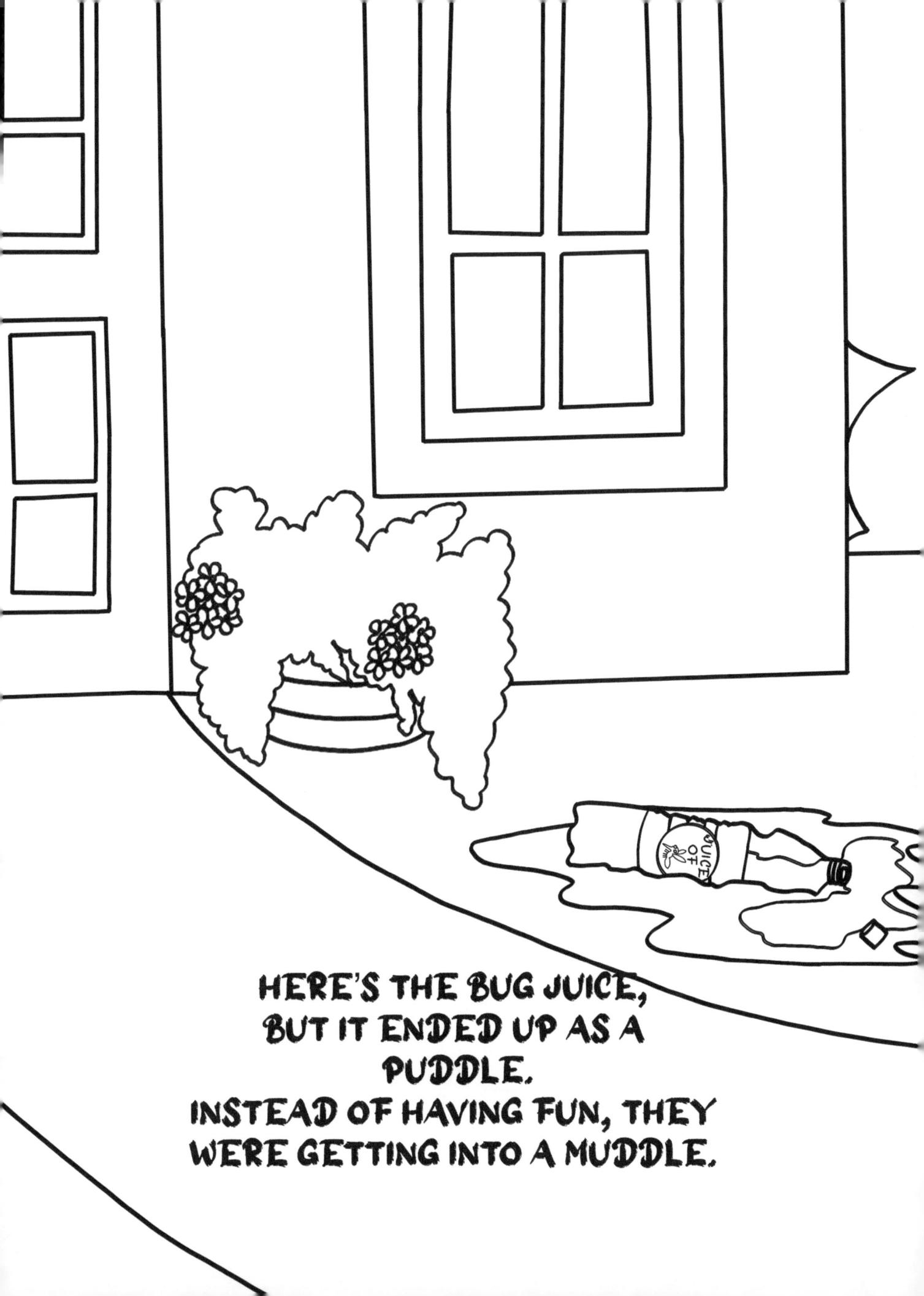

HERE'S THE BUG JUICE,
BUT IT ENDED UP AS A
PUDDLE.
INSTEAD OF HAVING FUN, THEY
WERE GETTING INTO A MUDDLE.

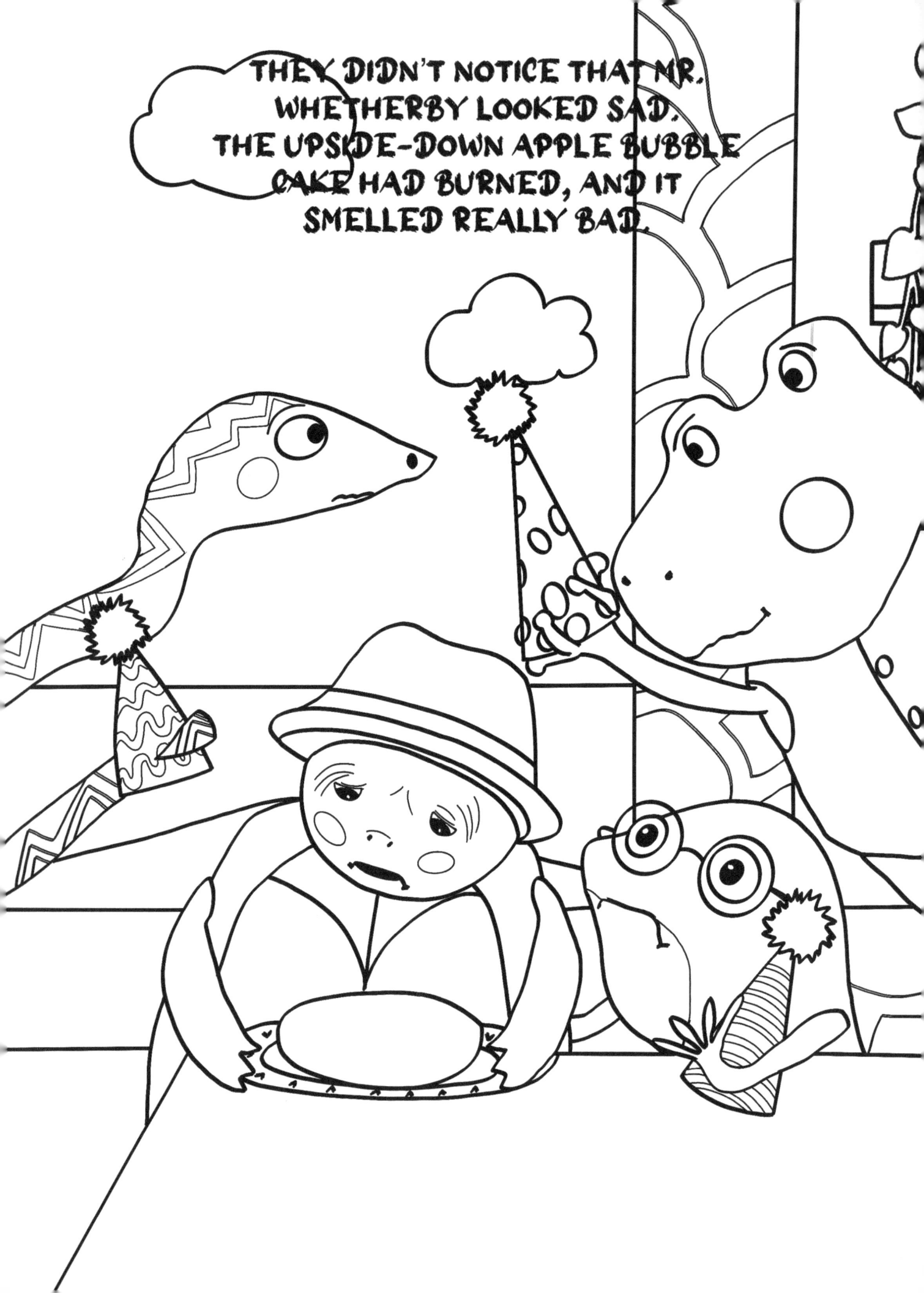

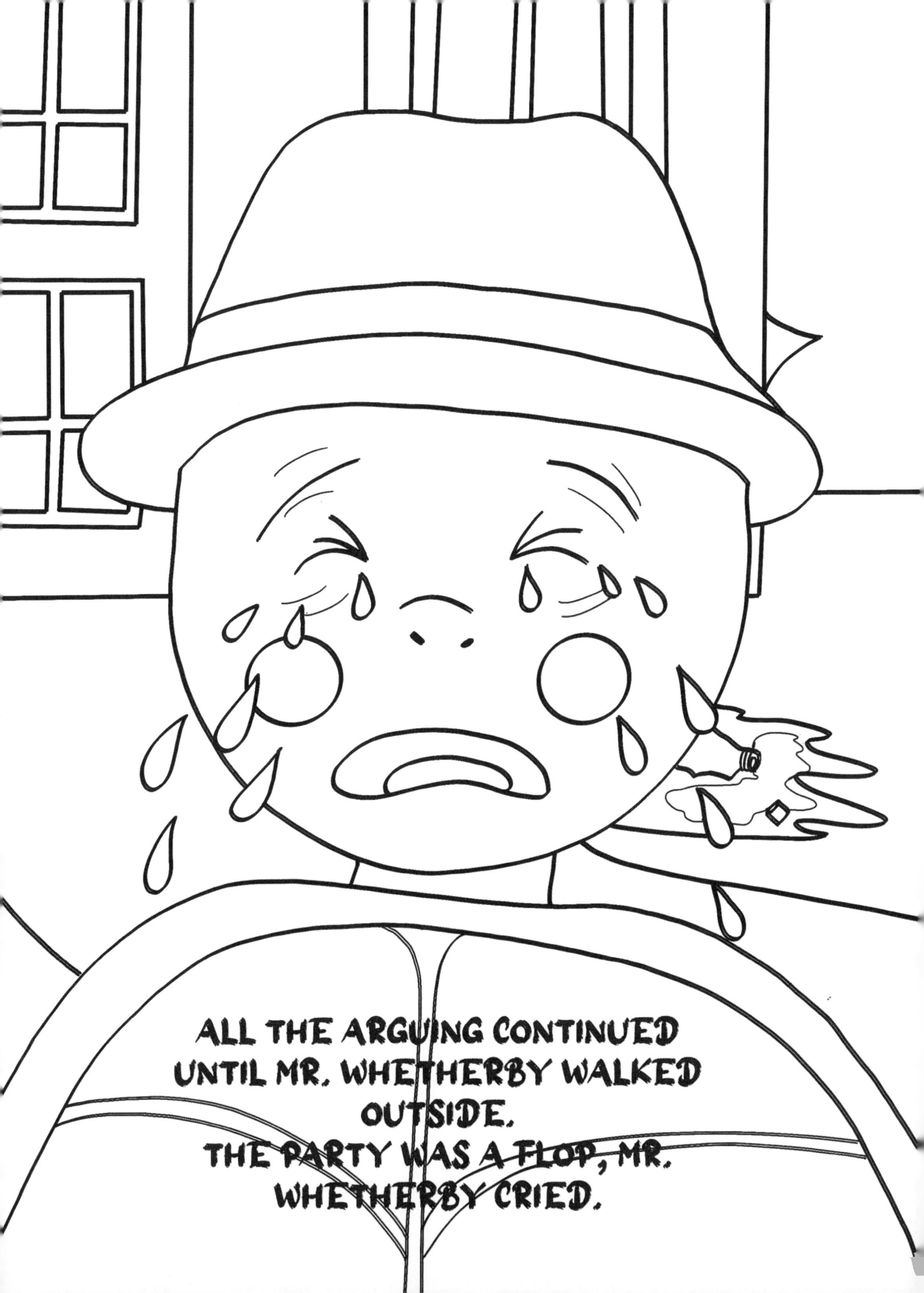

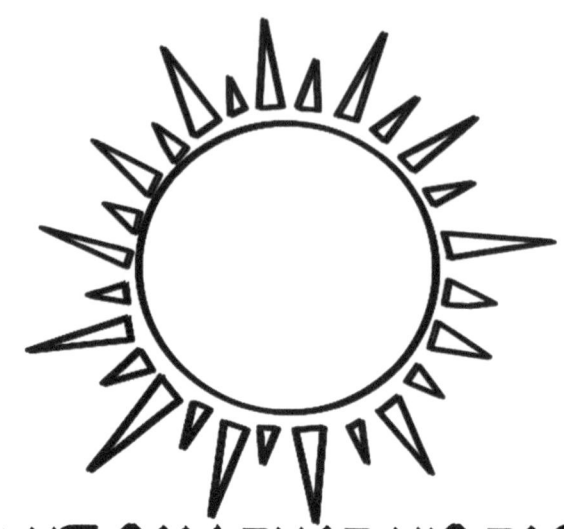

THEN HE SAW THAT HIS TABLE
WAS ALL SET IN HIS GARDEN.
HE WAS SO POLITE HE SAID,
"I BEG YOUR PARDON, BUT
WOULD YOU LIKE TO HAVE APPLE
MUFFINS AND TEA?"
IT'S SUCH A BEAUTIFUL DAY,
WON'T YOU JOIN ME?".

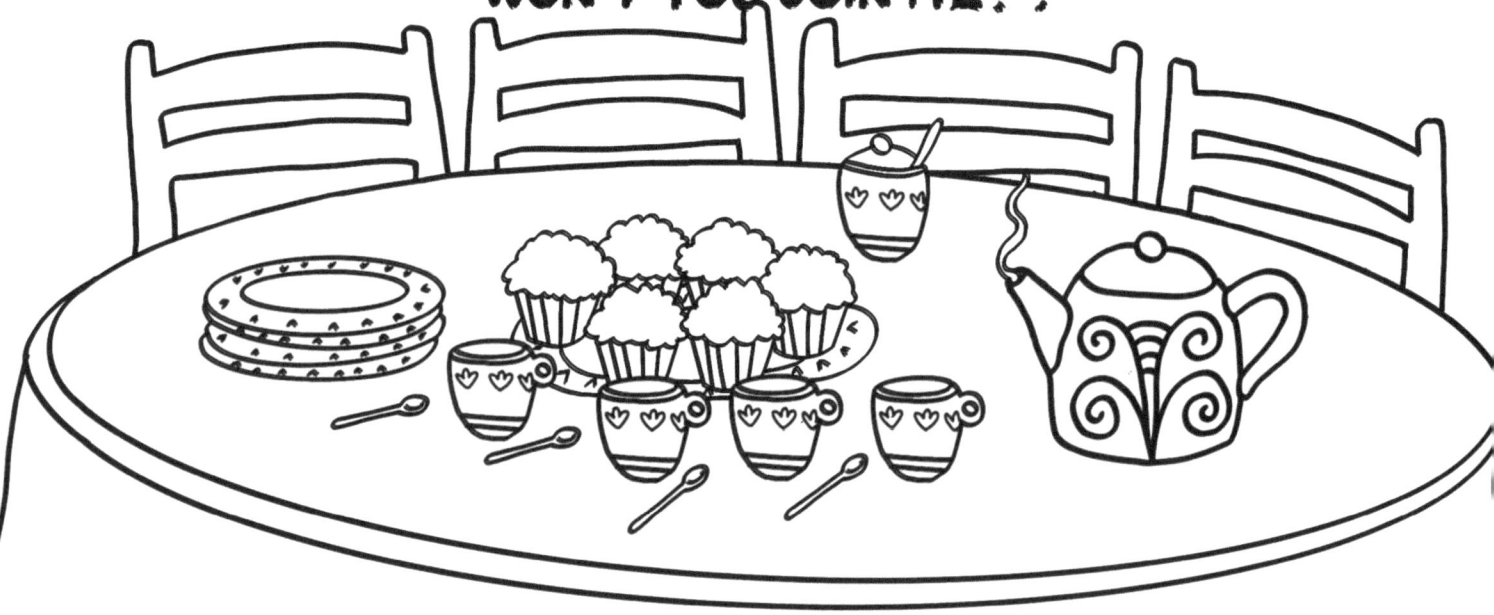

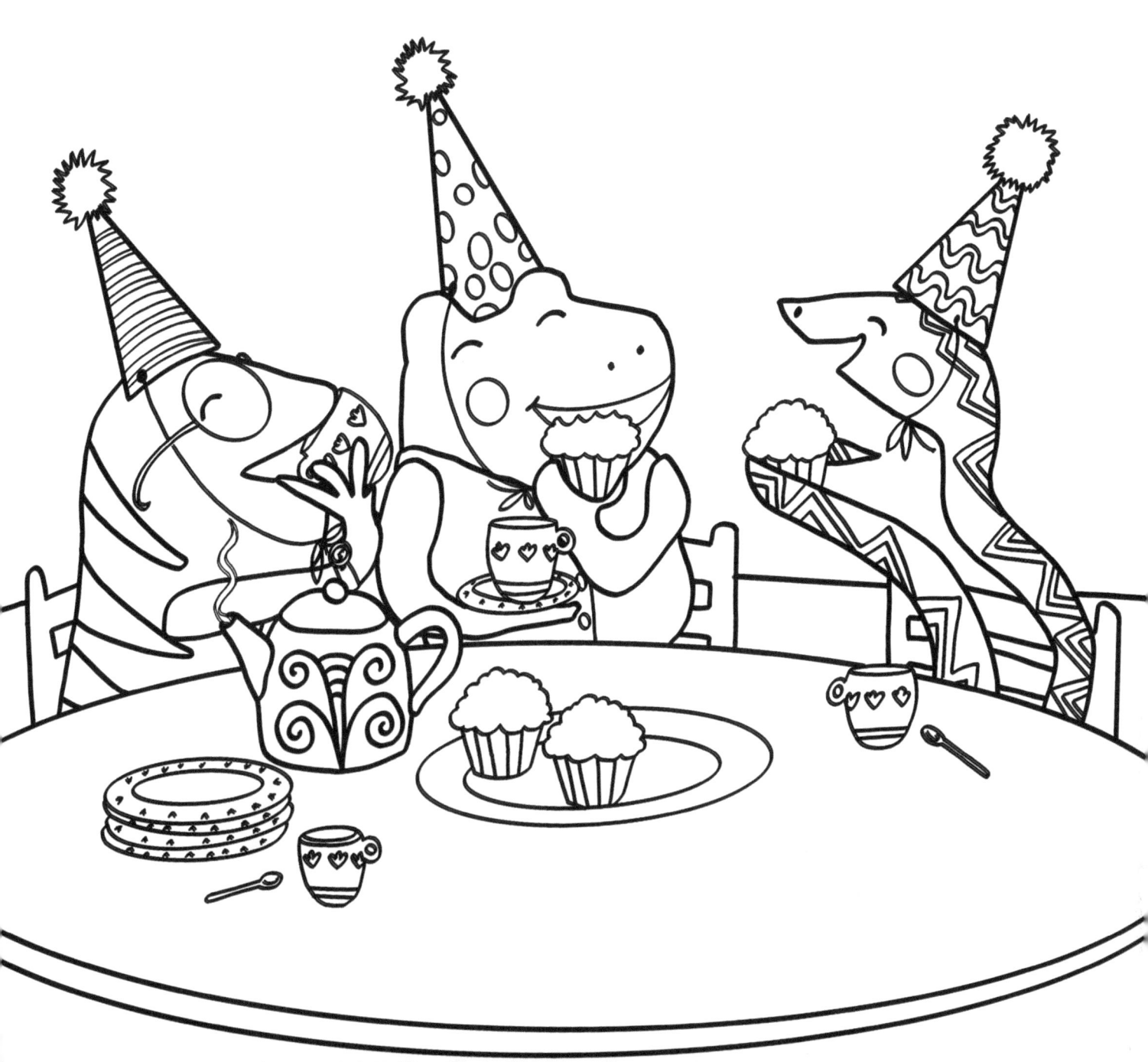

IT LOOKED SO DELICIOUS, THEY
ALL SAT DOWN.
THE FRIENDS WERE ALL HAVING
FUN; NOT A CONTRARY WORD
COULD BE FOUND.

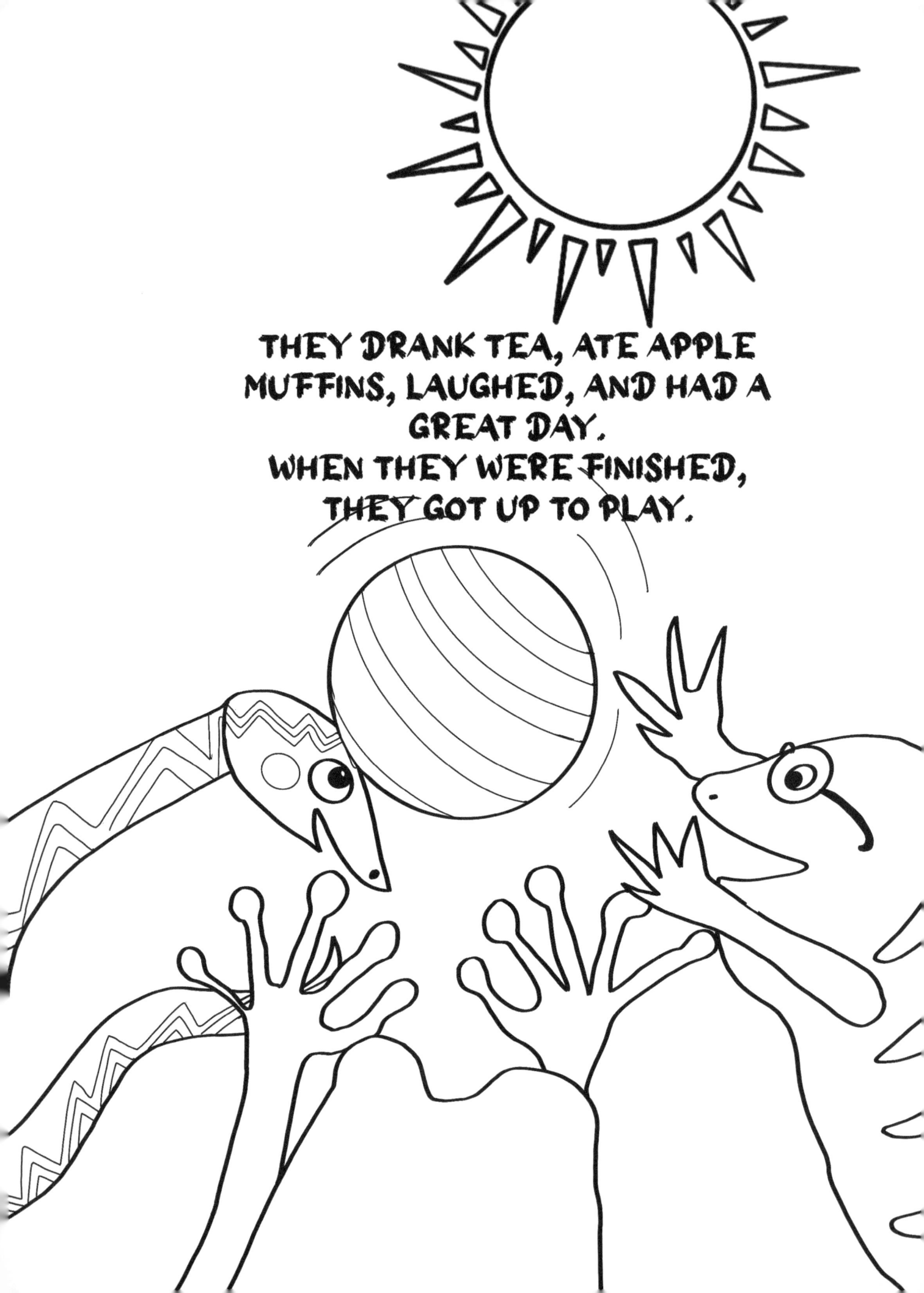

THEY DRANK TEA, ATE APPLE
MUFFINS, LAUGHED, AND HAD A
GREAT DAY.
WHEN THEY WERE FINISHED,
THEY GOT UP TO PLAY.

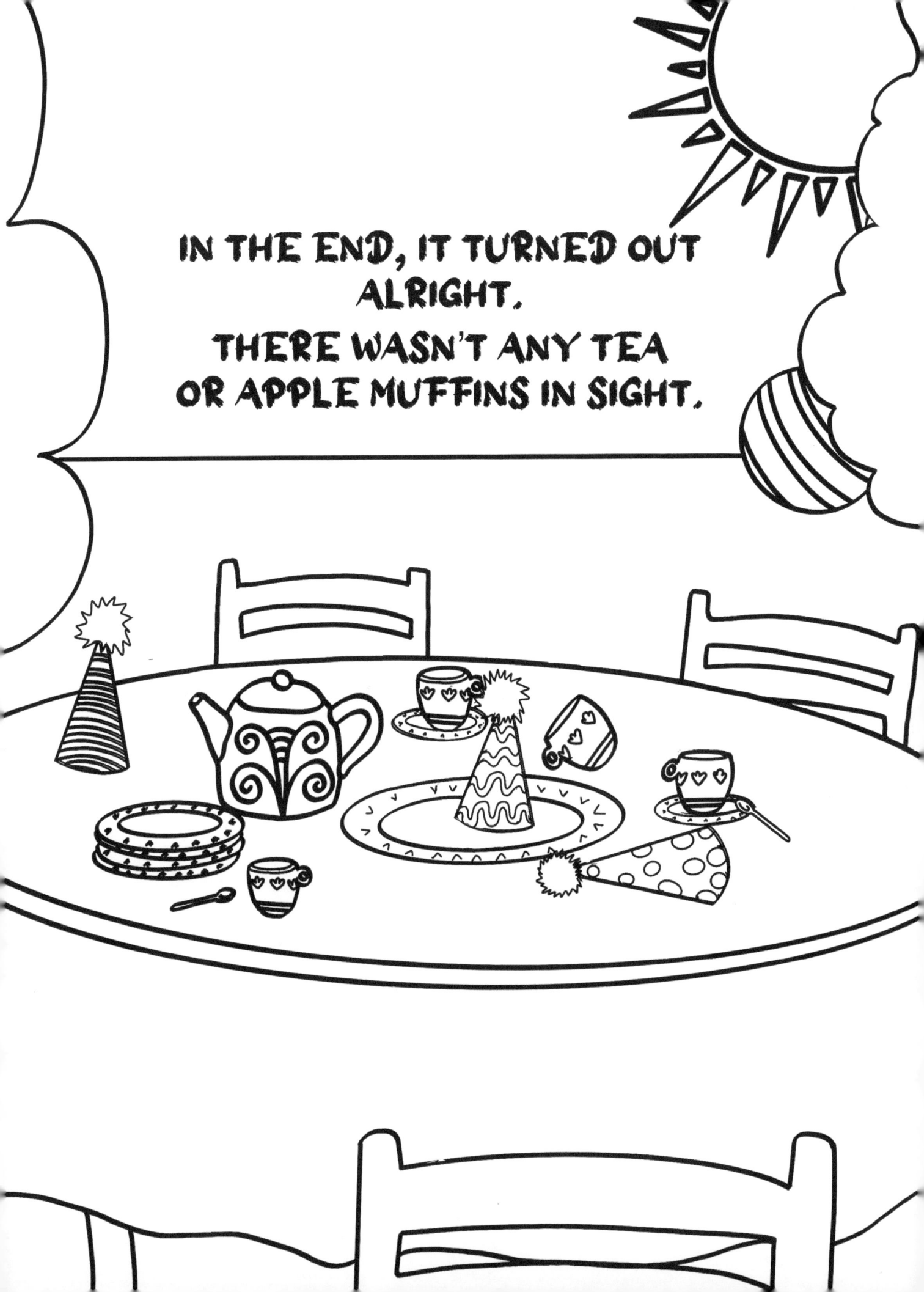

IN THE END, IT TURNED OUT ALRIGHT.
THERE WASN'T ANY TEA
OR APPLE MUFFINS IN SIGHT.

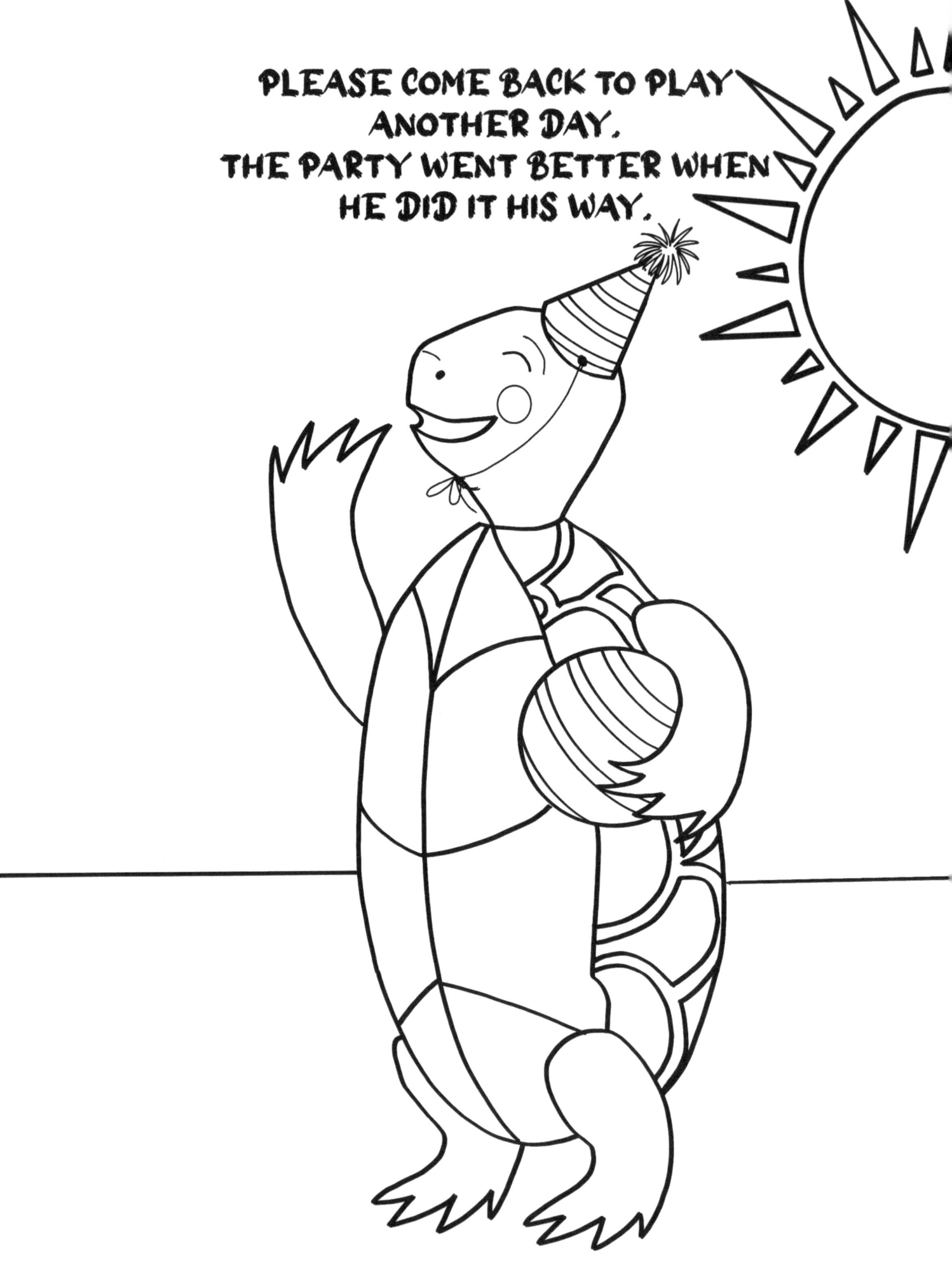

WHEN MR. WHETHERBY WAS
PUTTING HIS CUPS BACK ON THE
SHELF,
HE REALIZED THAT TODAY HE HAD
LEARNED TO THINK FOR HIMSELF.

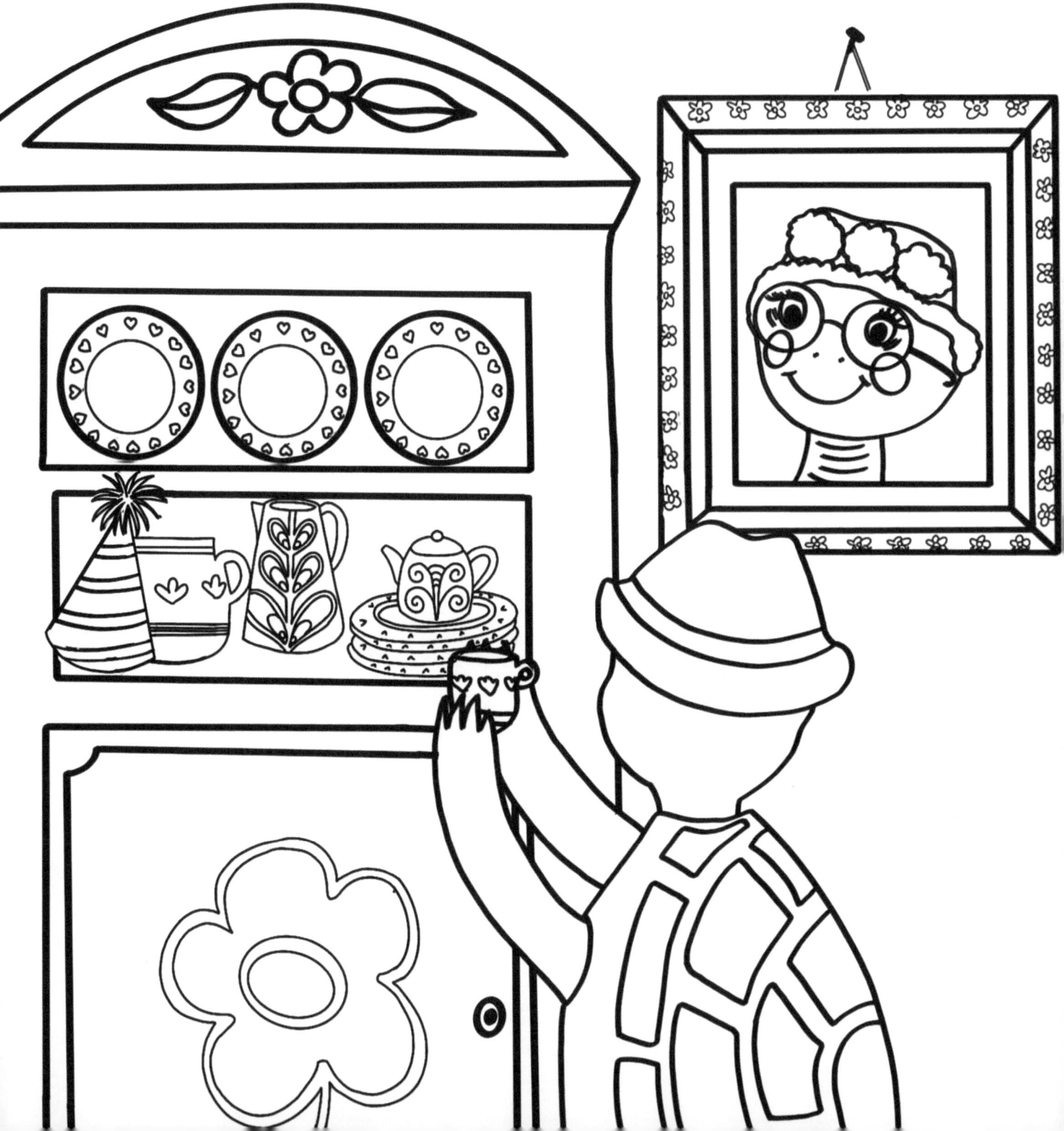